Sharing Family Stories and Memories

Prompts for Writing Your Memoirs for Future Generations

By
Lorine McGinnis Schulze

Publisher Olive Tree Genealogy
ISBN 978-1-987938-25-8

Dedication

To my children and grandchildren. I share my family stories and memories with them in order to preserve and pass them on to the next generation

Table of Contents

Why Record Your Memories?

It's important as genealogists that we not forget about writing our own story. Yes, we all want to find information on our ancestors and once we find it, many of us will share that information with other family members. But what about our own memories? We may think writing about ourselves is boring or egotistical but stop and think how excited you would be if you found a journal or memoirs that your great great grandmother kept!

I began my Life Story last year. I started with my first memory and tried to keep my journal chronological. It was a matter of writing down my memories of each year of my life. That soon proved to be very difficult. I got confused - had I written about my mother falling on the ice her first time skating? Or my father dressing up as Santa then giving out the wrong presents? I simply could not recall what I had already written and what was a memory that had just surfaced.

So after months of mulling on the problem I decided on a new method of writing my own life story. This new method keeps me on track, and helps me remember if I already wrote about a memory or not.

I write about my memories of the past - memories of my family (parents, grandparents, aunts, uncles and siblings), memories of special events, stories told by my parents or grandparents, my time at school, as a child, a teenager, an adult, newly married. Thus it is my life story and memories but by topics rather than chronological.

I invite you to begin your personal genealogy journey. Start your own journal and write your stories. Use the prompts in this book to jog your memory or guide you. Write daily or weekly or monthly, but write! Remember, family stories are lost over 3 generations unless they are recorded and preserved. Don't wait to start preserving your precious memories.

Where To Record Your Memories

Buy a good book to keep your Life Memories in if you are writing them by hand. I write in leather bound journals because I like how they feel and look important! They look like something that won't be tossed in the trash 50 years from now.

That's important because I'm writing my memories for my descendants - children, grandchildren, great grandchildren not yet born. So I don't want to write in something that could easily be discarded in the future simply because it doesn't look worth saving.

So choose a notebook that appeals to you and keep it handy.

A Few Tips Before You Begin

Combine facts (where you went to school, names of teachers, where you lived) as well as emotions - happy and sad. These are your memories so it's up to you to decide what you want to share but don't overlook the sad moments too.

Stay focused on the topic but jot down other memories that pop into your head as you are writing. You will be amazed at what memories surface as you are putting your thoughts down on paper. You can add those jot notes later when we get to a topic that fits.

Don't type your memories - writing them by hand gives your descendants a sense of YOU - your style, your emotions. Handwriting is a reflection of our personality.

Be sure you talk about your feelings about the memory. Describe the sights, the sounds, the smell – remember we use all our senses and describing your sense perceptions of each memory will make your stories come alive for those who will read them in the future.

As well as using the prompts in this book, you can look at old family photos to jog your memory of events or people. You could also talk to other family members for their input.

Choose a daily (or weekly or monthly) time period for your writing. If you get in the habit of writing at the same time each day, you will find your journal writing flows more easily. Write early morning with your cup of tea or coffee. Write just as you are going bed or after supper when the children have gone to bed. Whatever is a good quiet time for you. I try to set aside 30 minutes each day for writing my memories.

It is a good idea to begin with a brief outline of your family – names, dates and places of birth, marriage and death. Don't go back more than 3 generations – this isn't a huge family tree project, you just want to give your descendants an overview of who you are and who the members of your family are.

Sharing Memories Prompts & Topics

Not all of my prompts will apply to you. Some might not appeal to you. Others will hopefully remind you of some other episode that you can record. Remember these prompts are only meant to guide you or help jog your memory of your early years.

Your Family

This topic can be as simple as a list of people living in your home, or it can be more descriptive with details of personality traits for each person. Write whatever you think most important about each family member including their likes and dislikes, appearance, and so on.

Your Earliest Childhood Memory

How old were you? What do you remember – is the memory visual or sensory? Was it something pretty or horrible? Was it a scary memory or a happy one? Where did the memory happen? Were you inside or outside? Who was with you? What were your thoughts and feelings about this event or object?

Your Childhood Home or Homes

Describe each home you lived in. Give the address if you remember it. I like to draw a little sketch of the floor plan of each house I lived in as a child. Write down the names of your neighbors if you remember them. What did you like about each home? What didn't you like? Did you have a big yard or a tiny one? Perhaps you lived in an apartment rather than a house. How many rooms were there? Did you have your own bedroom or did you have to share? How was the home decorated – what kind of furniture did you have?

Your Childhood Town or City

Did you live in the country? In a city? In a small town or village? Describe your surroundings – how many hospitals, movie theatres, population and so on. What did you like about your town or city? What didn't you like?

Memories of Mom & Dad

Remembering Mother
You may break this into smaller topics or one long entry. Write about what kind of mother she was, a physical description, her hobbies, her occupation, is she still alive, when and where was she born, when and where did she marry your father, did she have siblings, was she close to her parents

Mom's Cooking
Many people say their mom was a great cook. Is that true of your mother? Perhaps she (like mine) was not fond of cooking.

Times Shared with Mom
Did you and your mom do anything special together? Did she teach you to knit or sew or quilt? Did she read books to you?

Memories of Dad
This may be similar to the topics you wrote about for your mother. Give a physical description of your father. Tell what his job was. What kind of father was he? What were his hobbies? What were his favorite things?

Times Shared with Dad
Did your father take you fishing or hunting? Did he play games with you? Maybe he played piano while you sang along.

Mom & Dad's Favorite Things
Did your mom and dad have items they purchased together that had pride of place in your home? Did they like to go dancing, or bowling? Maybe they both loved flowers or walks in the park.

Memories of Grandparents

If you spent time with your grandparents, this is where you will talk about what you remember or overheard. Talk about each one in turn and describe your feelings about them.

Grandfathers

Describe your grandfathers. What did they look like? What kind of personalities did they have – happy? Grumpy? Crusty? Fun? What was their job? Where and when were they born?

Grandpa Time

Did your grandfathers do any fun things with you? Did they play cards with you or show you how to build things or bait a hook with a worm?

Grandmothers

Describe your grandmothers. What did they look like? What did they were? What was Grandma's favorite color? What kind of personalities did they have – happy? Fun? Were they warm and fuzzy or aloof? Did they work outside the home? Where and when were they born?

Grandma's Stories

Did either of your grandmothers tell you stories of their childhood or their parents? It's important to write those memories and stories down before they are lost.

Memories of Your Siblings

Talk about your brothers and sisters if you had any. What were they like? How much older or younger were they? What is the most vivid memory you have of each sibling? Did you get along or did you fight all the time? Did you have a favorite sibling or one you were closest to? Did you share a bedroom with a sibling?

If you were an only child talk about what that was like. Did you miss not having siblings? Or were you glad you were the only one to get your parents' attention?

Memories of Other Relatives

In this section you can write about relatives you knew – cousins, aunts, uncles and other family members. Use the topics below to guide you.

Who Was Your Favorite Relative?

It's okay to write about a favorite relative – in your journal you can say what it was that made you like being around them. Were they lots of fun? Maybe they had interesting stories to tell?

Relatives I Wish I'd Known Better

Perhaps your grandparents' siblings were close to your grandparent but you never had much of a chance to chat with them. This is your chance to tell what you remember or what your grandparents told you about a sibling or other relative.

Visiting other Family Members

Did you visit other relatives very often? Did they visit you? You may want to talk about one or two visits that stand out in your mind. Perhaps your Dad got lost on the way to your Grandmother's house, or the car broke down or Grandma was still in her housecoat.

Family Life in General

Going to the dentist
Describe your emotions before a dental visit. What smells and sounds do you remember? Talk about one or two specific visits that stick out in your mind, whether a good memory or a traumatic one. How often did you go to the dentist?

Going to the Doctor
Can you recall going to the doctor as a child? Talk about some specific instances and describe your feelings, the sights, the sounds and the smell. Who took you? Why were you going?

The Library
Did your parents take you to the local library? Did they belong to a library? What was the attitude about reading in your home?

Activities outside your home
What kinds of activities were you encouraged to participate in? Sports? Art? Dance? Music?

Bedtime Routines
Every family has its own routines. What was the typical bedtime routine in your home?

Special Moments
Choose a few special moments that you remember fondly. Describe them – how old were you, who was part of the moment, where were you.

Sad Moments
Life is a mix of happiness and sadness. For your journal to be authentic you should include the sad memories too. Perhaps a pet died. Perhaps someone you loved moved away, got sick or died.

Happy Times

You should choose a few happy times to talk about in your journal. Describe those times – who was with you, how old were you, where were you and how did you feel?

Church

Did your family attend church? What denomination? Describe the church you went to and how often you attended services.

Community Events

Did you take part in Community Events such as parades or celebrations? Maybe you always went to annual festivities that are often held in communities. Describe the crowds, the atmosphere, your feelings and what you remember most.

Trips & Adventures

Did you go on many family trips? Perhaps you went to the cottage every summer. Pick a couple of episodes of life at the cottage that stand out for you the most and describe them. Perhaps it was going to the outhouse or the noises at night. Maybe you went camping – what did the tent smell like? Who cooked and how?

Childhood Pets

Did you have a dog or a cat or another pet? Maybe you had goldfish or a hamster or a bird or a pet snake. Talk about your pets – their names, their personalities and how you felt about them. What was fun and what was work?

Games You Played With Friends
Describe the games that were popular in your childhood. Which did you play? Hopscotch? Hide and Seek?

Games You Played With Your Siblings
This was likely very different games from those you played with friends. Did you play Indian Leg Wrestling? Tiddlywinks? Board games?

Naughty Things You Did as a Kid
Time to 'fess up! Pick one or two naughty things you did and describe them. Were you found out? What was your punishment?

Friends You Had
This could be a simple list of names or you might want to describe your friends in detail.

Favorite TV Shows
Did you have a television? What shows did you watch? What was your favorite? Why did you like it best?

Favorite Books
What were your favorite books? Why?

Broken Bones & Other Accidents
Did you ever break any bones? How did it happen? Where? Did you go to the hospital? Describe what your visit to the doctor or hospital was like.

Weekly Traditions
Did your family have weekly traditions such as Movie Night or Games Night? Describe those traditions in general but then pick one or two that stand out in your mind and write about them in detail. Maybe you played cards every Friday night – what games did you play, who played with you, what snacks did you have?

Imaginary Friends
Did you have an imaginary friend? Many children did. Who was yours? What was his or her name? Was it a person or an animal? When was the first time you remember having your imaginary friend and when (and how) did they disappear from your life?

Stuffed Animals or Cuddle Blanket You Loved
Many children sleep with a stuffed animal, or carry one around during the day. Some have a favorite cuddle blanket and can't sleep without it. Describe yours if you had one. Tell what happened to it.

Sleepovers
Did you have sleepovers at your house? Or did you go to sleepovers at other friend's homes? Who was there? What did you do? How often did you go or have one? Pick a few funny or disastrous times that stand out in your mind and describe what happened

Sweet Sixteen
Girls often had a sweet sixteen birthday party. Did you have anything special on your 16th birthday?

Things That Go Bump in the Night
Did you suffer from night terrors or nightmares? Were you afraid of the dark? Maybe you were scared of monsters under the bed or ghosts in your closet. Tell about these night fears and describe your feelings if you can remember them. How did you solve your fear?

Childhood Illnesses
What childhood illnesses did you come down with? Did you have the measles, mumps, chicken pox, croup or other illnesses? Or were you vaccinated for them? What do you remember about these illnesses?

Childhood Pranks

Were you a prankster, or a practical joker? Maybe a sibling played jokes on you. Tell about any pranks in your journal and be sure to tell who was involved and whether or not it was funny.

Your Childhood Pets

What pets did you have as a child – cats, dogs, fish, birds, or something more exotic? Give their names and describe what they looked like. What part of their care and feeding was your responsibility?

Your Friends

Most of us have a few best friends. Make a list of all the friends you remember and then describe one or two of your best friends in detail. What were they like? What did you do together? How long were you friends?

Lessons

Did you take any lessons as a child? Maybe you took music lessons, or swimming or art or dance or skating lessons. Talk about the lessons your parents made you take and the lessons you wanted to take.

Teenage Years

Getting Your Driver's Licence
Who taught you to drive? What kind of car was it? How old were you? Do you remember going to take the driving test? What was it like? How did you do?

Teen Hangouts
Some towns had special places for teenagers. If your town or city had one, describe it in your journal. If there was no designated spot, what were some of your friends' teen hangouts – the local drugstore? A diner? A community center? Where did you and your buddies go and what did you do there?

Dances
When did you learn to dance and what kind of dancing did you do? Were there regular dances held in your community? Did you go to school dances? What about Sadie Hawkins dances – did you ever attend one? Who did you ask to be your date? Pick a memorable moment or two from a dance – something funny or embarrassing or awesome, and tell about it.

Boyfriends & Girlfriends
Okay now's your chance to talk about your boyfriends, especially that first one. Give names (remember your descendants are going to want to know who you were in love with before you married their grandfather or great-grandfather!) How did you meet, how long were you boyfriend-girlfriend? What smell or song do you associate with them?

Girlfriends (Besties)
Who were your best friends? Did you have one bestie or many? Record their names in your journal and describe them in detail – physical, personality, where they lived, how old they were and so on. Talk about what you liked to do together – did you tell each other your innermost secrets? Did you style each other's hair?

Fashion

What were the fashions when you were growing up? What did you wear? What did an older sibling wear? What about your mom and dad – what did they wear? What was in and what was out?

Hair

What hair styles were in when you were young? How did you wear yours? What color was your hair? Was it wavy, curly or poker straight? Was it easy to style your hair in the current fashion or did you have to iron it on an ironing board to straighten it? Maybe you wore curlers to bed every night or scotch-taped your bangs to make them curl.

Interests

What did you like to do? Were you involved in sports? Did you like to sing or dance or play a musical instrument? Were you a social butterfly or more of a solitary person? Did you belong to any clubs or take part in any organized activities?

Weekends

What kinds of things did you do on the weekends? Did you go to the beach? Maybe you went to the Saturday matinees or the drive-in. Did you hang out at the local burger place? Did you explore the country or go skinny-dipping in the local creek? Maybe you had a part-time job on Saturdays?

After-school job

Did you work after school? Where did you work and what did you do there? How old were you when you started working after school and how often did you have to work? How much did you get paid? Did you like your job or hate it? Who else worked with you and who was your boss. Make sure you record as many names as you can and give a description and address of where you worked if possible. Your descendants will want to know all the details.

Fun Times

What did you do for fun? What were fun times for you and your friends? Did you go bowling? Hang out at the local drugstore soda counter?

Music

What was popular in music when you were a teenager? What singers and bands did you listen to? Did you have posters of singers or rock stars on your bedroom walls? Did you ever attend a live concert? Did you buy lots of records or did you grow up in the era of 8-track?

Local Diners & Jukeboxes

Did you have a local diner that was "the" place to be? Did you grow up in the era of jukeboxes? What did the cool kids do and where did they hang out? Were you part of that group?

Embarrassing Moments

We've all had them. That horrible moment when the mustard from your hotdog falls on your white top when you're trying to impress someone. When you spend all day out with friends then come home to find you have something stuck between your teeth. When you wore two different shoes by mistake for a job interview. Pick one moment that was truly embarrassing and talk about it in your journal.

Family Rules & Expectations

The Telephone
What kind of telephone did your family have? How many phones were in your house? Was it a party line? A rotary dial? What color was it? Do you remember your phone number? Were you allowed to use the phone to chit chat with your friends or was it for emergencies and "important" calls only?

Car Rides
What kind of car did your family own? Where did everyone sit – were there arguments over who got a window seat? Who drove – mom or dad? Did mom have her own car? Think of an interesting, funny or scary car ride you had as a kid and write about it.

Meal Times
What was the usual routine at meal times? Did your family eat all 3 meals together? Or did you fend for yourselves? Where did everyone sit at the table? Did you have your own spots and that is where you all sat every day? Did you eat in a dining room or in the kitchen? What were the smells and sounds at the dinner table or in the kitchen during meals? Pick one or two meal times that stand out in your memory and share them in your journal. Maybe it was a special occasion meal such as Thanksgiving or Christmas and perhaps your siblings fought over who was getting the drumstick?

Air Raid Sirens & Curfew
Did you have a curfew? What time did you have to be home or in bed? Did your town or village have a curfew. Mine had an air raid siren that went off at dark and that signalled curfew and all teens to head home.

Bedtime
Did your mom and dad follow a bedtime routine? Did they read you a story or allow you to read for awhile before lights out? What was the routine leading up to going to bed – snack? TV?

Did you have a night light or was it dark in your bedroom? What time was bedtime?

Discipline
How did your parents handle discipline? Did they believe in spankings or did they use other methods of consequences for bad behavior? Did you have lots of rules or very few? Were your parents lenient or strict? Who handled discipline?

Chores
What kind of chores did you and your siblings have to do? Did you wash dishes, set tables, take out garbage, do the ironing, look after younger siblings, dust, vacuum, make your bed, or wash floors? Or did mom and dad do everything? Were the household chores divided by gender, did boys do "boy" chores and girls do "girl" chores?

School Life

Your Schools
Where did you go to school? What were the schools like – a one-room schoolhouse or a large city school? Describe each of your schools and how many pupils were in each. How many teachers were there? Who was the principal of each school you attended?

Grade Levels
Did you start school with Kindergarten? How old were you when you started school? In your journal you will want to talk about each grade as a separate topic – Kindergarten, 1, 2, 3, 4, 5, 6, 7, 8, 9, 10, 11, 12, 13 (if you had Grade 13 in your country), College, University and so on. Who was your teacher? Did you like that teacher? Did you like the grade you were in? Did you dislike it and if so, why? Who were some of the other students in each class? What do you remember most about each grade?

Favorite Subject
You may want to talk about your favorite subject in each grade you were in, but also write about your all-round favorite subject. If you have old report cards, refer to them to jog your memory. Consider copying them out into your journal or scanning them and adding them as photos.

Extra-Curricular Activities
Did you participate in activities after school? What were they? What grades were you in for each activity? What did you enjoy the most? Were you in school sports, or music or did you write for the school newspaper?

Your Favorite Teachers
Make a list of your favorite teachers and what grade each taught. Which one was your absolute favorite and why? What made you list the teachers you chose?

Summer Holidays

What were your summer holidays like? Was your mom a stay-at-home mother and you spent your days with her, or did you go to a sitter or to grandma's house. What kinds of things did you do during the summer to keep busy? Did you play with friends, go swimming, go hiking or camping or boating? Perhaps you had a summer job. What did you like best about summer? What did you dislike?

March or Spring Break
Did you go anywhere special on March break? Did your family plan trips together during that week?

Back to School
Were you excited about going back to school after summer holidays or did you dread going back to class in September? Did you get new clothes for school? Did you get new school supplies?

Graduations
Share your graduation memories in your journal. Did you win any awards? Were you a valedictorian? Did you go to any parties after Graduation?

Prom Night
If you had a prom describe what you wore and who you went with. Were you excited? Happy? Nervous? Was it your first prom? Describe the setting and give the names of anyone you remember being there. What music was played? Was there a live band? What kind of dancing did you do? Help your descendants feel the magic of prom night with a full description – sounds, sights, smells and your emotions.

Firsts

What were some of the firsts in your life? There will no doubt be happy firsts and sad firsts – first kiss, first death for example. In this section you will want to describe each first in detail. How old were you? How did you feel? Where were you? Who else was involved? What do you remember about your surroundings – sights, sounds, smells....

First Bike
How old were you? What kind of bike was it? What color? Who gave it to you? How much did it cost? What kind of experience was it the first time you hopped on and rode it? Who taught you to ride?

First Car
When did you get your first car? Did you buy it or was it a gift from someone? How much did it cost and what was the make? What color was it? What do you remember about the car's interior – did it have a radio, CD player, 8 Track Tape Deck, seat belts? Was it gear shift or automatic? What was the first drive like and where did you go?

First Dance
How old were you when you had your first dance? Who was your dance partner and where was it? What were you wearing? Were you nervous or excited? Did your hands sweat or were you calm and collected?

First Movie
What was the first movie you saw in the movie theatre? How old were you? Was it with your parents, with friends, or alone? Did you go to movies all the time or was it a special treat?

First Kiss
I'm sure you remember your first kiss! How old were you and who did you kiss? Where were you and what happened after the kiss?

First Crush
Who was your first crush? Was it the boy/girl next door? An older classmate? Write about your crush in your journal and be sure to provide the name and other details – appearance, personality, how old you were.

First Death in the Family
Do you remember the first relative to pass away in your family? Here's a chance to write a memorial to that relative. You will want to tell how old you were and how the death occurred.

First Wedding in the Family
Who was the first (that you remember) in your family to be married? Was it an older sibling? A cousin? Were you in the wedding party? How old were you? Who did they marry and where? What year was the wedding? Describe the wedding venue and reception if you were there. Were you excited about the wedding? Perhaps you were not actually at the service or reception but you can still record your memories of what other family members said or did.

First Time a Bridesmaid or Groomsman
Have you been in a wedding party as a bridesmaid, flower girl, ring bearer, usher or groomsman? Describe your duties and what you wore. Do you remember the flowers and how they smelled? What was the venue like? Who was getting married and where? How old were you?

First Airplane Ride
How old were you when you first flew in an airplane? Where were you going? Who was with you? Were you excited or nervous? What was the flight like? Describe the inside of the plane, and the stewardesses. Were you served food? If so, what was it. What kind of plane was it? How many passengers or seats did the plane carry? Did anything eventful happen on the flight?

First Summer or After-School Job
How old were you when you got your first summer or after-school job? What was the job? Where was it? How much were you paid? How many hours did you have to work each week? When did you work – evenings, weekends, after-school, Monday to Friday all day in the summer? Why did you get your job and what did you do with the money? Were you saving up for something special or spending it?

First Full Time Job
How old were you when you were first hired full-time? What was the job and where was it? What did you do in your job? Did you like the job or hate it? Were you still living at home or had you moved out to your own place? Who were some of your fellow employees? Who was your boss? What kind of atmosphere was it at work? How long did you work there?

First Heartache
Who was it? When was it? How did it happen? How long did it take you to get over it?

Special Holidays & Traditions

Depending where you live and what religion you are, you will have special holidays that I have not listed here. In Canada we celebrate July 1st which is Canada Day. In the United States, July 4th is a very important holiday. Feel free to create your own list and just use this category to jog your memory of family Holiday Times.

In your Journal describe how your family observed each of these holidays. What special foods did you eat? Did you stay up past your regular bedtime? Did you wear special clothes or go to church or visit other family members? What exciting or fun moment do you remember about each special day?

Be sure to give a general overview of your holiday traditions but also think of a few special moments in each holiday that really stand out for you. Write about those few outstanding moments – perhaps Mom and Dad only got coal in their Santa stockings one Christmas, or Mom dropped the Thanksgiving turkey.

Christmas
Did you get a Christmas stocking? When did you get to open it? Did you go to midnight mass or observe some other religious ceremony? When did your family open gifts and how was it done – did everyone open at once or did you go in some kind of order such as youngest to oldest? Did you have a special Christmas morning breakfast or supper? Did you visit relatives on Christmas Day or did any come to your home? Did your family play Christmas carols or sing them and if so, which ones were your favorite?

Santa Claus Parade
Did you see the Santa Claus parade every year? How far away was it? How old were you when you stopped going? What was the day like? What did you like best about the parade? Was there anything you didn't like about it? Who took you? What was the

weather like? What sounds and sights do you recall from the parade?

Easter
What were the usual Easter traditions in your home? Did Easter Bunny visit and leave candy and gifts? Did you have an Easter egg hunt? Did you go to church? Write about the overall traditions but then pick one or two Easter memories that stand out in your mind and talk about them in detail.

Thanksgiving
What was a traditional meal that you had on Thanksgiving? Did you celebrate with family in your home or elsewhere? What was your favorite part of the day and your favorite part of the meal? Pick one or two special Thanksgivings and talk about those in detail.

Hallowe'en
Here is your chance to think about the Hallowe'en costumes you wore over the years. What is the first Hallowe'en you remember? How old were you when you started going Trick or Treating? What candies do you remember getting? What was your usual routine for Halowe'en? What was the weather usually like on Hallowe'en? Pick one or two special Hallowe'en days or nights and talk about those in detail.

July 1st
What is your most vivid memory of this Canadian holiday? Do you know the history of this celebration? What traditions did your family observe on this day? Did you have special foods and barbeques? Did you purchase a new flag for your car or home?

July 4th
What is your most vivid memory of this American holiday? Do you know the history of this celebration? What traditions did your family observe on this day? Did you have special foods and barbeques? Did you purchase a new flag for your car or home?

Remembrance Day / Memorial Day
How was Remembrance (Memorial) Day celebrated in your
home? What is your most vivid memory of that day? Did you
honor any soldiers in your own family on that day? Did you visit
cemeteries or cenotaphs to pay your respects?

Valentine's Day
Was Valentine's Day celebrated by your mom and dad? What
tradition was followed?

New Year's Celebrations
Do you remember what your parents did to celebrate New Year's
Eve? Did they go out with friends, or to a party or did they stay at
home to watch television? Did you celebrate as a family or were
you in bed long before midnight?

Boxing Day
What kinds of special things did your family do on Boxing Day?
Did they rush off to stores to get bargains? Were friends or
family invited for a special brunch? Or was it pretty much just
another day?

Birthdays
What was a typical birthday celebration like in your home? Did
you have a party, a cake with candles and gifts? Did your mom
make you a special meal?

Family Reunions
Did your family hold Family Reunions? Do you remember going
to any or having them at your home? What relatives did you
meet? What were your impressions of the reunion?

Father's Day
Did you do anything special for your dad or Grandpa on Father's
Day celebrations?

Mother's Day

Did you do anything special for your mom or Grandmother on Mother's Day celebrations? Did you make her breakfast in bed, give her a coupon for housework you would do for her?

Cooking & Meals

It's always fun to read about what great-grandma cooked and what kinds of appliances she had to do her cooking. This is your chance to talk about what it was like at your house or at your grandparents' home. The following questions are meant to trigger your memories from the past:

Was your mom a good cook? What were mom's specialties? Or did your dad do most of the cooking? Do you have any of your mother's or grandmother's recipes? What was a typical supper at your house? What did the family eat for breakfast and lunches?

What appliances were in your kitchen? Did mom use an ice-box or did she have a refrigerator? What about her stove? Was it electric or an old-fashioned coal or wood burning stove? Did your mom or grandmother make pickles or preserves? What did the kitchen smell like when food was being cooked? What was your favorite meal? Did you like the foods your parents' prepared?

Childhood Myths

Talk about your memories of Santa, Easter Bunny or the Tooth Fairy. What other myths do you remember?

Santa Claus

What are some special memories you have of visiting Santa? Did you get a stocking from Santa or his Elves? When did you open it – at night or first thing in the morning? What was the most awesome stocking stuffer you can remember getting? How old were you when you found out that Santa didn't exist? How did that make you feel?

The Tooth Fairy

Do you remember how you felt when you put your tooth under your pillow at night? How much money did the Tooth Fairy leave? When and how did you learn that there was no such thing as the Tooth Fairy?

The Easter Bunny

Did Easter Bunny bring gifts? What were they?

Favorite Things

Your Favorite Activities
Did you like to draw? To color? Sing or Dance? Did you like to build things? Did you love sports? Maybe you liked to read. Describe what you did, where and how often.

Your Favorite Books
List your favorite books you read as a child. Why did you like them?

Your Favorite Songs
What were your favorite songs as a young child or a teenager? Did you memorize all the words? Was there one song that held a special meaning for you?

Your Favorite Movie
What was your favorite movie and why? How old were you when you watched it?

Favorite Toy
Did you love your yo-yo or your slinky or your rubber ball? Maybe it was a skipping rope or a doll or truck that you held dear. How old were you when you got the toy? Who gave it to you?

Favorite Game
Did you like to play Hide & Seek with the neighborhood kids? Maybe you loved a different game like Hop-Scotch. Talk about whatever game you loved best and tell why you loved it.

Your Favorite T.V. Show
Did you have a favorite TV Show? Was it a western, a cartoon or something else.

Your Favorite Meal

What meal did you like the best? What was it that you enjoyed about it? Did mom make it very often? What did it smell like and how was it served?

Seasonal Family Times

In this section you can write about family life during each of the 4 seasons – Spring, Summer, Winter and Fall (Autumn). Each season brings its own traditions – winter meals versus summer meals. The weather is very different for each season and that affects activities and fun times.

Some of the topics for each season that you could write about are:

Seasonal Meals
What were some of the winter meals you had as a family? Did you barbeque in the summer or go on picnics? Was summer a time for mom to make preserves or put up pickles for the winter?

Seasonal Weather
Describe the kind of weather that was typical for each of the seasons in your area. If you can recall, try to write about some weather that stand out for you, such as a torrential rain or mudslides in the spring. Perhaps you remember a winter so severe that you had to ski to school.

Seasonal Vacations
Did your family go on vacations in the summer or winter? Some families liked to take a vacation on March break or at Christmas. Pick one or two outstanding memories of a seasonal vacation and describe them in your journal.

Seasonal Activities
Every season has its own special activities. Winter can be snowshoeing, skiing, tobogganing, sleigh rides and skating if you lived where there is snow. Summer can be swimming, going to the beach, biking, hiking and camping. What were some of the activities that you and your family took part in each season? Did you garden in the spring and summer, then harvest your bounty in the fall?

Adult Memories

Leaving Home
How old were you when you left home to be on your own? Or did you leave home to marry? Where did you live once you left home? Were you still geographically close to your parents or were you far away? Did you leave home to go to college or university or to get a job?

Careers and Jobs you have had
If you have a resume (CV) use it to help jog your memory of different jobs you have had. Describe each job and whether or not you enjoyed it. What did you learn from your jobs?

Family Feuds
Were there any feuds in your family? Who was involved and were they ever resolved?

Your Wedding
Who did you marry? Give a description of your spouse including personality. How and where did you meet? Describe your wedding attire and what your attendants wore. Where did you marry? When? Who were the guests? What was the day like and what is your one special memory of that day?

Historical Events
Do you remember the man on the Moon, 9/11, Cuban Missile Crisis, Vietnam, Korean War, Cold War, Assassinations, Changes for Women, Changes for African-Americans or other historical events? Talk about them – your memories, your feelings (fear, joy and so on) and how others reacted.

Miscellaneous

Births, Baptisms, Marriages, Deaths, Burials

What births and baptisms took place in your family when you were young? Do you remember any? What marriages took place in your family? Perhaps Gramma married for the third time? This is your place to write the details and provide the names of extended family who were born, baptised, married or died. Did you attend a funeral or a church christening? Write the details in your journal and provide your descendants more fascinating information about your family. Remember to talk about the sounds and smells and your emotions of a specific event. That helps bring your story alive.

Soldiers in Your Family

Was your family a military family? Were any of your siblings or other relatives involved in any wars? Your journal is your opportunity to remember and honor them.

Extreme Weather

Have you lived through extreme weather such as earthquakes, tornadoes, lightning strikes, floods, mudslides, blizzards, hurricanes, thunderstorms, hail, cyclone or other?

Hobbies & Crafts

What are some of the hobbies or crafts you, your siblings, your parents or grandparents enjoyed? Maybe you had an aunt who was an amazing artist or quilter. Perhaps your dad played harmonica in a local amateur band. Did your grandpa build model trains? Write down your memories of the hobbies and crafts you or your family took part in.

Lessons

Did you take lessons as a child? Some that come to mind are music (example guitar, piano, accordion), dance (example jazz, tap, ballet), Art, Sports (example skating, swimming, hockey) Write down your memories of any lessons you took – what were they, who was your teacher, how old were you, where were they held, did you enjoy them or hate them, tell about practise time.

The Milkman Cometh
Do you remember when milk and bread was delivered to your door? Talk about those experiences – how old were you, what sounds did you hear when the milkman walked up the sidewalk?

Laundry Day
Did your mom use a wringer-washer? Do you remember what it was like? Did you get to use it too? How long did it take to wash clothes? Did she use a laundromat? Did she have a modern electric dryer or did she hang clothes on the clothesline?

Changes in Technology
What are some of the changes in technology that you have seen in your lifetime? Telephones look different and have gone from rotary dial to touch tone. Car phones – remember the first ones that came out? And of course cell phones and smartphones are amazing changes in technology. How about records to tapes to CD to iPod? Computers comes to mind – were there personal computers when you were a child? You might want to describe some of the changes – what was your first computer and how old were you?

Point-form Outline of Prompts

The following is a brief outline of the prompts you read in my book. I hope this will help you follow along as you begin your own story. You can easily go back into a specific chapter to refresh your memory of the questions and suggestions I've presented for each prompt and topic.

Why Record Your Memories?

Where To Record Your Memories

A Few Tips Before You Begin
- Combine facts
- Stay focused on the topic
- Don't type your memories - write them by hand
- Talk about your feelings
- Use the prompts in this book to help you
- Look at old family photos to jog your memory
- Choose a daily (or weekly or monthly) time period for your writing.
- Begin with a brief outline of your family

Prompt: Your Family

Prompt: Your Earliest Childhood Memory

Prompt: Your Childhood Home or Homes

Prompt: Your Childhood Town or City

Prompt: Memories of Mom & Dad

- Remembering Mother
- Mom's Cooking
- Times Shared with Mom
- Memories of Dad
- Times Shared with Dad

- Mom & Dad's Favorite Things

Prompt: Memories of Grandparents

- Grandfathers
- Grandpa Time
- Grandmothers
- Grandma's Stories

Prompt: Memories of Your Siblings

Prompt: Memories of Other Relatives
- Who Was Your Favorite Relative?
- Relatives I Wish I'd Known Better
- Visiting other Family Members

Prompt: Family Life in General
- Going to the dentist
- Going to the Doctor
- The Library
- Activities outside your home
- Bedtime Routines
- Special Moments
- Sad Moments
- Happy Times
- Church
- Community Events
- Trips & Adventures
- Childhood Pets

Prompt: Childhood Days
- Games You Played With Friends
- Games You Played With Your Siblings
- Naughty Things You Did as a Kid
- Friends You Had
- Favorite TV Shows
- Favorite Books

- Broken Bones & Other Accidents
- Weekly Traditions
- Imaginary Friends
- Stuffed Animals or Cuddle Blanket You Loved
- Sleepovers
- Sweet Sixteen
- Things That Go Bump in the Night
- Childhood Illnesses
- Childhood Pranks
- Your Childhood Pets
- Your Friends
- Lessons

Prompt: Teenage Years

- Getting Your Driver's Licence
- Teen Hangouts
- Dances
- Boyfriends & Girlfriends
- Girlfriends (Besties)
- Fashion
- Hair
- Interests
- Weekends
- After-school job
- Fun Times
- Music
- Local Diners & Jukeboxes
- Embarrassing Moments

Prompt: Family Rules & Expectations

- The Telephone
- Car Rides
- Meal Times
- Air Raid Sirens & Curfew
- Bedtime
- Discipline
- Chores

Prompt: School Life
- Your Schools
- Grade Levels
- Favorite Subject
- Extra-Curricular Activities
- Your Favorite Teachers
- Summer Holidays
- March or Spring Break
- Back to School
- Graduations
- Prom Night

Prompt: Firsts
- First Bike
- First Car
- First Dance
- First Kiss
- First Crush
- First Death in the Family
- First Wedding in the Family
- First Time a Bridesmaid or Groomsman
- First Movie
- First Airplane Ride
- First Summer or After-School Job
- First Full Time Job
- First Heartache

Prompt: Special Holidays & Traditions
- Christmas
- Santa Claus Parade
- Easter
- Thanksgiving
- Hallowe'en
- July 1st
- July 4th
- Remembrance Day / Memorial Day
- Valentine's Day

- New Year's Celebrations
- Boxing Day
- Birthdays
- Family Reunions
- Father's Day
- Mother's Day

Prompt: Cooking & Meals

Prompt: Childhood Myths
- Santa Claus
- The Tooth Fairy
- The Easter Bunny

Prompt: Favorite Things
- Your Favorite Activities
- Your Favorite Books
- Your Favorite Songs
- Your Favorite Movie
- Favorite Toy
- Favorite Game
- Your Favorite T.V. Show
- Your Favorite Meal

Prompt: Seasonal Family Times
- Seasonal Meals
- Seasonal Weather
- Seasonal Vacations
- Seasonal Activities

Prompt: Adult Memories
- Leaving Home
- Careers and Jobs you have had
- Family Feuds
- Your Wedding
- Historical Events

Prompt: Miscellaneous

- Births, Baptisms, Marriages, Deaths, Burials
- Soldiers in Your Family
- Extreme Weather
- Hobbies & Crafts
- Lessons
- The Milkman Cometh
- Laundry Day
- Changes in Technology